THE JPS B'NAI MITZVAH
TORAH COMMENTARY

Pekudei (Exodus 38:21–40:38)
Haftarah (1 Kings 7:51–8:2)

Rabbi Jeffrey K. Salkin

The Jewish Publication Society · Philadelphia
University of Nebraska Press · Lincoln

INTRODUCTION

News flash: the most important thing about becoming bar or bat mitzvah isn't the party. Nor is it the presents. Nor even being able to celebrate with your family and friends—as wonderful as those things are. Nor is it even standing before the congregation and reading the prayers of the liturgy—as important as that is.

No, the most important thing about becoming bar or bat mitzvah is sharing Torah with the congregation. And why is that? Because of all Jewish skills, that is the most important one.

Here is what is true about rites of passage: you can tell what a culture values by the tasks it asks its young people to perform on their way to maturity. In American culture, you become responsible for driving, responsible for voting, and yes, responsible for drinking responsibly.

In some cultures, the rite of passage toward maturity includes some kind of trial, or a test of strength. Sometimes, it is a kind of "outward bound" camping adventure. Among the Maasai tribe in Africa, it is traditional for a young person to hunt and kill a lion. In some Hispanic cultures, fifteen year-old girls celebrate the *quinceañera*, which marks their entrance into maturity.

What is Judaism's way of marking maturity? It combines both of these rites of passage: *responsibility* and *test*. You show that you are on your way to becoming a *responsible* Jewish adult through a public *test* of strength and knowledge—reading or chanting Torah, and then teaching it to the congregation.

This is the most important Jewish ritual mitzvah (commandment), and that is how you demonstrate that you are, truly, bar or bat mitzvah—old enough to be responsible for the mitzvot.

What Is Torah?

So, what exactly is the Torah? You probably know this already, but let's review.

The Torah (teaching) consists of "the five books of Moses," sometimes also called the *chumash* (from the Hebrew word *chameish,* which means "five"), or, sometimes, the Greek word Pentateuch (which means "the five teachings").

Here are the five books of the Torah, with their common names and their Hebrew names.

> **Genesis (The beginning), which in Hebrew is Bere'shit (from the first words—"When God began to create").** Bere'shit spans the years from Creation to Joseph's death in Egypt. Many of the Bible's best stories are in Genesis: the creation story itself; Adam and Eve in the Garden of Eden; Cain and Abel; Noah and the Flood; and the tales of the Patriarchs and Matriarchs, Abraham, Isaac, Jacob, Sarah, Rebekah, Rachel, and Leah. It also includes one of the greatest pieces of world literature, the story of Joseph, which is actually the oldest complete novel in history, comprising more than one-quarter of all Genesis.

> **Exodus (Getting out), which in Hebrew is Shemot (These are the names).** Exodus begins with the story of the Israelite slavery in Egypt. It then moves to the rise of Moses as a leader, and the Israelites' liberation from slavery. After the Israelites leave Egypt, they experience the miracle of the parting of the Sea of Reeds (or "Red Sea"); the giving of the Ten Commandments at Mount Sinai; the idolatry of the Golden Calf; and the design and construction of the Tabernacle and of the ark for the original tablets of the law, which our ancestors carried with them in the desert. Exodus also includes various ethical and civil laws, such as "You shall not wrong a stranger or oppress him, for you were strangers in the land of Egypt" (22:20).

> **Leviticus (about the Levites), or, in Hebrew, Va-yikra' (And God called).** It goes into great detail about the kinds of sacrifices that the ancient Israelites brought as offerings; the laws of ritual purity; the animals that were permitted and forbidden for eating (the beginnings of the tradition of kashrut, the Jewish dietary laws); the diagnosis of various skin diseases; the ethical laws of holiness; the ritual calendar of the Jewish year; and various agricultural laws concerning the treatment of the Land of Israel. Leviticus is basically the manual of ancient Judaism.

- Numbers (because the book begins with the census of the Israelites), or, in Hebrew, Be-midbar (In the wilderness). The book describes the forty years of wandering in the wilderness and the various rebellions against Moses. The constant theme: "Egypt wasn't so bad. Maybe we should go back." The greatest rebellion against Moses was the negative reports of the spies about the Land of Israel, which discouraged the Israelites from wanting to move forward into the land. For that reason, the "wilderness generation" must die off before a new generation can come into maturity and finish the journey.

- Deuteronomy (The repetition of the laws of the Torah), or, in Hebrew, Devarim (The words). The final book of the Torah is, essentially, Moses's farewell address to the Israelites as they prepare to enter the Land of Israel. Here we find various laws that had been previously taught, though sometimes with different wording. Much of Deuteronomy contains laws that will be important to the Israelites as they enter the Land of Israel—laws concerning the establishment of a monarchy and the ethics of warfare. Perhaps the most famous passage from Deuteronomy contains the *Shema,* the declaration of God's unity and uniqueness, and the *Ve-ahavta,* which follows it. Deuteronomy ends with the death of Moses on Mount Nebo as he looks across the Jordan Valley into the land that he will not enter.

Jews read the Torah in sequence—starting with Bere'shit right after Simchat Torah in the autumn, and then finishing Devarim on the following Simchat Torah. Each Torah portion is called a parashah (division; sometimes called a *sidrah,* a place in the order of the Torah reading). The stories go around in a full circle, reminding us that we can always gain more insights and more wisdom from the Torah. This means that if you don't "get" the meaning this year, don't worry—it will come around again.

And What Else? The Haftarah

We read or chant the Torah from the Torah scroll—the most sacred thing that a Jewish community has in its possession. The Torah is written without vowels, and the ability to read it and chant it is part of the challenge and the test.

But there is more to the synagogue reading. Every Torah reading has an accompanying haftarah reading. Haftarah means "conclusion," because there was once a time when the service actually ended with that reading. Some scholars believe that the reading of the haftarah originated at a time when non-Jewish authorities outlawed the reading of the Torah, and the Jews read the haftarah sections instead. In fact, in some synagogues, young people who become bar or bat mitzvah read very little Torah and instead read the entire haftarah portion.

The haftarah portion comes from the Nevi'im, the prophetic books, which are the second part of the Jewish Bible. It is either read or chanted from a Hebrew Bible, or maybe from a booklet or a photocopy.

The ancient sages chose the haftarah passages because their themes reminded them of the words or stories in the Torah text. Sometimes, they chose *haftarah* with special themes in honor of a festival or an upcoming festival.

Not all books in the prophetic section of the Hebrew Bible consist of prophecy. Several are historical. For example:

The book of Joshua tells the story of the conquest and settlement of Israel.

The book of Judges speaks of the period of early tribal rulers who would rise to power, usually for the purpose of uniting the tribes in war against their enemies. Some of these leaders are famous: Deborah, the great prophetess and military leader, and Samson, the biblical strong man.

The books of Samuel start with Samuel, the last judge, and then move to the creation of the Israelite monarchy under Saul and David (approximately 1000 BCE).

The books of Kings tell of the death of King David, the rise of King Solomon, and how the Israelite kingdom split into the Northern Kingdom of Israel and the Southern Kingdom of Judah (approximately 900 BCE).

And then there are the books of the prophets, those spokesmen for God whose words fired the Jewish conscience. Their names are immortal: Isaiah, Jeremiah, Ezekiel, Amos, Hosea, among others.

Someone once said: "There is no evidence of a biblical prophet ever being invited back a second time for dinner." Why? Because the prophets were tough. They had no patience for injustice, apathy, or hypocrisy. No one escaped their criticisms. Here's what they taught:

> God commands the Jews to behave decently toward one another. In fact, God cares more about basic ethics and decency than about ritual behavior.
> God chose the Jews *not* for special privileges, but for special duties to humanity.
> As bad as the Jews sometimes were, there was always the possibility that they would improve their behavior.
> As bad as things might be now, it will not always be that way. Someday, there will be universal justice and peace. Human history is moving forward toward an ultimate conclusion that some call the Messianic Age: a time of universal peace and prosperity for the Jewish people and for all the people of the world.

Your Mission—To Teach Torah to the Congregation

On the day when you become bar or bat mitzvah, you will be reading, or chanting, Torah—in Hebrew. You will be reading, or chanting, the haftarah—in Hebrew. That is the major skill that publicly marks the becoming of bar or bat mitzvah. But, perhaps even more important than that, you need to be able to teach something about the Torah portion, and perhaps the haftarah as well.

And that is where this book comes in. It will be a very valuable resource for you, and your family, in the b'nai mitzvah process.

Here is what you will find in it:

> A brief **summary** of every Torah portion. This is a basic overview of the portion; and, while it might not refer to everything in the Torah portion, it will explain its most important aspects.
> A list of the **major ideas** in the Torah portion. The purpose: to make the Torah portion real, in ways that we can relate to. Every Torah portion contains unique ideas, and when you put all

of those ideas together, you actually come up with a list of Judaism's most important ideas.

> Two **divrei Torah** ("words of Torah," or "sermonettes") for each portion. These *divrei Torah* explain significant aspects of the Torah portion in accessible, reader-friendly language. Each *devar Torah* contains references to **traditional** Jewish sources (those that were written before the modern era), as well as **modern** sources and quotes. We have searched, far and wide, to find sources that are unusual, interesting, and not just the "same old stuff" that many people already know about the Torah portion. Why did we include these minisermons in the volume? Not because we want you to simply copy those sermons and pass them off as your own (that would be cheating), though you are free to quote from them. We included them so that you can see what is possible—how you can try to make meaning for yourself out of the words of Torah.

> **Connections:** This is perhaps the most valuable part. It's a list of questions that you can ask yourself, or that others might help you think about—any of which can lead to the creation of your *devar Torah.*

Note: you don't have to like everything that's in a particular Torah portion. Some aren't that loveable. Some are hard to understand; some are about religious practices that people today might find confusing, and even offensive; some contain ideas that we might find totally outmoded.

But this doesn't have to get in the way. After all, most kids spend a lot of time thinking about stories that contain ideas that modern people would find totally bizarre. Any good medieval fantasy story falls into that category.

And we also believe that, if you spend just a little bit of time with those texts, you can begin to understand what the author was trying to say.

This volume goes one step further. Sometimes, the haftarah comes off as a second thought, and no one really thinks about it. We have tried to solve that problem by including a **summary** of each haftarah, and then a mini-sermon on the haftarah. This will help you learn how these sacred words are relevant to today's world, and even to your own life.

All Bible quotations come from the NJPS translation, which is found in the many different editions of the JPS TANAKH; in the Conservative movement's *Etz Hayim: Torah and Commentary;* in the Reform movement's *Torah: A Modern Commentary;* and in other Bible commentaries and study guides.

How Do I Write a *Devar Torah?*

It really is easier than it looks.

There are many ways of thinking about the *devar Torah.* It is, of course, a short sermon on the meaning of the Torah (and, perhaps, the haftarah) portion. It might even be helpful to think of the *devar Torah* as a "book report" on the portion itself.

The most important thing you can know about this sacred task is: *Learn* the words. *Love* the words. Teach people what it could mean to *live* the words.

Here's a basic outline for a *devar Torah:*

"My Torah portion is (name of portion) _____,
    from the book of _____ , chapter
    _____.

"In my Torah portion, we learn that_____
    (Summary of portion)

"For me, the most important lesson of this Torah portion is (what
    is the best thing in the portion? Take the portion as a whole;
    your *devar Torah* does not have to be only, or specifically, on the
    verses that you are reading).

"As I learned my Torah portion, I found myself wondering:
    ➤ *Raise a question that the Torah portion itself raises.*
    ➤ *"Pick a fight"* with the portion. Argue with it.
    ➤ *Answer a question* that is listed in the "Connections" section of
       each Torah portion.
    ➤ *Suggest a question to your rabbi* that you would want the rabbi
       to answer in his or her own *devar Torah* or sermon.

"I have lived the values of the Torah by _____
(here, you can talk about how the Torah portion relates to your
own life. If you have done a mitzvah project, you can talk about
that here).

How To Keep It from Being Boring
(and You from Being Bored)

Some people just don't like giving traditional speeches. From our per-
spective, that's really okay. Perhaps you can teach Torah in a different
way—one that makes sense to you.

> Write an "open letter" to one of the characters in your Torah por-
tion. "Dear Abraham: I hope that your trip to Canaan was not too
hard . . ." "Dear Moses: Were you afraid when you got the Ten
Commandments on Mount Sinai? I sure would have been . . ."
> Write a news story about what happens. Imagine yourself to
be a television or news reporter. "Residents of neighboring cities were horrified yesterday as the wicked cities of Sodom and
Gomorrah were burned to the ground. Some say that God was
responsible . . ."
> Write an imaginary interview with a character in your Torah portion.
> Tell the story from the point of view of another character, or a mi-
nor character, in the story. For instance, tell the story of the Gar-
den of Eden from the point of view of the serpent. Or the story
of the Binding of Isaac from the point of view of the ram, which
was substituted for Isaac as a sacrifice. Or perhaps the story of
the sale of Joseph from the point of view of his coat, which was
stripped off him and dipped in a goat's blood.
> Write a poem about your Torah portion.
> Write a song about your Torah portion.
> Write a play about your Torah portion, and have some friends act
it out with you.
> Create a piece of artwork about your Torah portion.

The bottom line is: Make this a joyful experience. Yes—it could
even be fun.

The Very Last Thing You Need to Know at This Point

The Torah scroll is written without vowels. Why? Don't *sofrim* (Torah scribes) know the vowels?

Of course they do.

So, why do they leave the vowels out?

One reason is that the Torah came into existence at a time when sages were still arguing about the proper vowels, and the proper pronunciation.

But here is another reason: The Torah text, as we have it today, and as it sits in the scroll, is actually *an unfinished work.* Think of it: the words are just sitting there. Because they have no vowels, it is as if they have no voice.

When we read the Torah publicly, we give voice to the ancient words. And when we find meaning in those ancient words, and we talk about those meanings, those words jump to life. They enter our lives. They make our world deeper and better.

Mazal tov to you, and your family. This is your journey toward Jewish maturity. Love it.

THE TORAH

❖ Pekudei: Exodus 38:21–40:38

And, now, the book of Exodus comes to an end. Despite the fact that this book takes its name from the Exodus from Egypt, leaving Egypt is not the most important thing that happens in that biblical book. Judging from the sheer amount of ink that the ancient scribes used in writing the book, the most important thing that happens in Exodus is that the Israelites receive the "blueprint" for the Tabernacle, and then they build it. Pekudei contains a tally of all the precious metals that were used in its construction, along with detailed descriptions of how the priestly garments were made. It contains explicit instructions for how to set up the Tabernacle, with the refrain "just as the Lord had commanded Moses."

Finally, we read that God's presence filled the Tabernacle. Only when the cloud of God's presence lifted could the Israelites continue on their journeys.

Summary

> ‣ There is a detailed account of the weight and value of all the gold and silver used in the construction of the Tabernacle. (38:21–25)
> ‣ There is a detailed description of all the materials used in the priestly garments. (39:1–30)
> ‣ Moses sets up the Tabernacle as God had commanded. The language used in describing this project—"work," "completed," and "blessed"—echoes the language that the book of Genesis used when God created the world. (40:17–33)
> ‣ God's cloud, the visible sign of God's presence, descends upon the Tabernacle and becomes a signal for the People of Israel to move forward on their journey through the wilderness. (40:34–38)

The Big Ideas

- **Judaism demands accountability from both leaders and regular people.** Moses demands exact records of all the precious metals used in the building of the Tabernacle because he wanted to be sure no one would think he had taken some of the precious metals and kept them for himself. This teaches us that leaders must be exacting and deliberate in their public dealings, so that they will always remain above suspicion of corruption. The same goes for all of us.

- **Religious leadership is special, but not overly special.** Just as there needed to be an exact accounting of all the materials used in the construction of the Tabernacle, there needed to be an accounting of all the materials used in the design of the priests' garments. The garments themselves were considered holy, just as the priests were holy. By describing the garments in such detail, perhaps the authors of the Torah were trying to ensure that later generations would not decide to make the priestly garments even more special than they were intended to be. That is why the text keeps repeating "just as the Lord had commanded Moses."

- **There is a linkage between the creation of the Tabernacle and the creation of the world.** The Tabernacle is actually a model for the way that the world should exist—a place where people join together in community and show their gratitude to God. It is, or at least it was at that time, the only place where everything can unfold according to God's plan.

- **God is not stationary, sitting on a throne in heaven.** God wanders with the Jewish people. This idea sustained the Jewish people through centuries of exile. Wherever Jews have gone, wherever Jews have lived, no matter what: God has been in exile with us. God will not abandon us.

Divrei Torah

JEWISH LIVING CAN BE IN-TENTS

That was a bad pun. Sorry about that. But it does have something to teach us.

The place where the Israelites encountered God was called the *ohel mo'ed,* the Tent of Meeting. Not a house. Not a palace. But a tent.

This makes total sense. When you read the stories of Genesis, you see that the ancestors of the Jewish people were nomads who wandered from place to place, much like modern-day Bedouins in the Middle East. When you read the stories of Exodus, Leviticus, Numbers, and Deuteronomy, you get the same notion: the Israelites are always wandering, always on a journey. You might have heard the term "the wandering Jew." Actually, it is not a nice term. It was meant as an insult. It comes from an old Christian belief that God condemned the Jews to wander the earth.

Jews certainly don't believe that. And yet, for much of Jewish history, in many places and times, it has been true.

So, what is the significance that the place where God meets the Israelites is called a tent? By definition a tent is a temporary dwelling (just like the sukkah). That's the point. God doesn't simply "sit" in one place. God "wanders" with the Jewish people.

Throughout Jewish history, Jews have believed that *shekhinta bagaluta,* "the presence of God," is somehow in exile with them. Ever since the destruction of the Temples in Jerusalem, first by the Babylonians and then by the Romans, God has been in exile with the Jews. That idea sustained the Jews and comforted them through their years of wandering. God will not abandon them. In several midrashim, God not only wanders with the Jews; God shares in their pain and even (if you can imagine this) weeps with the Jews. Our religious structures are not always permanent. But our relationship with God is permanent. And God is with us in our distress and in our triumphs as well.

In our tradition God's presence is also likened to a fire. God is said to speak with Moses out of a burning bush, which burned and was not consumed. God is said to speak with the people at Sinai, which the Torah says burned with fire. Think of all the candles of Jewish living that we light: Shabbat candles, *Havdalah* candles, Hanukkah candles, and yahrzeit candles, and most of all, the *ner tamid*, the "eternal light." They all symbolize God's presence among us.

In the words of renowned contemporary commentator Avivah Zornberg: "The Book of Exodus ends with the people contemplating that fire. They see it as the fire of the Presence of God, a version of the fire of Sinai. The couple—God and the people—needs no candle, for the pillar of fire accompanies them in their exits and entrances."

CREATION—OR RE-CREATION?

You have probably had this experience: your parents or teachers speak to you about something, and then, a week later or so, they repeat the same thing. And you probably find that boring.

But not every repetition is boring. Sometimes, we can learn a lot from it.

Consider this last portion of the book of Exodus. It describes the building of the ancient Tabernacle in painstaking detail. But when we read it, we realize something. The language of the instructions sounds familiar. We read similar language at the very beginning of the Torah when we read the account of the world's creation.

Follow the parallels: Moses examines the handiwork of the Tabernacle. In the creation story, God sees all that God has made and finds it very good. God finds creation to be meaningful, just like the Tabernacle will be meaningful.

There is more: "And when Moses saw [*vayar*] that they had performed all the tasks [*kol ha-melakhah*]—as the Lord had commanded, so they had done [*asu*]—Moses blessed them" (39:43). To the attentive reader, the links to the creation story are unmistakable: "And God saw [*vayar*] all [*kol*] that God had done [*asah*], and it was very good" (Gen. 1:31). In the one case, God looks and sees, while in the other Moses does; in both cases, everything has been completed, just as God wants.

So, are the creation of the world and the creation of the Tabernacle exactly the same? No. God single-handedly created the world. But God gives human beings the task of building the Tabernacle. This is similar to the Jewish mystical idea of *tzimtzum,* which means "to limit" or "to reduce." If God fills all space, how could the world have come to be? God had to "shrink" in order to make room for the world to exist. In a similar way, leaders must make themselves "smaller" in order for their followers to actually do the right thing. It is true of teachers, coaches—and especially parents. In modern psychological terms, we must limit our ego in order to let others grow.

As the contemporary Jewish thinker Eugene B. Borowitz teaches: "Take the case of a parent who has the power to insist upon a given decision and a good deal of experience upon which to base that judgment. In such an instance, the urge to compel is almost irresistible. Yet if it is a matter the parent feels the child can handle—better, if making this decision and taking responsibility for it will help the child grow—then the mature parent withdraws and makes it possible for the child to choose."

So, just as God didn't build the Tabernacle, but let Moses do it, sometimes human beings have to step back and let others learn and grow. Your parents will do this for you, and you will do it for others.

Connections

➤ In what way does God "wander" the world with the Jewish people?

➤ What are some of the places where God "lives?"

➤ In what ways have you had to be accountable—to parents, teachers, and yourself?

➤ Have you ever had the experience of *tzimtzum*—of parents, teachers, or coaches "withdrawing" from a task in order for you (or others) to grow? What was it like?

THE HAFTARAH

❖ Pekudei: 1 Kings 7:51–8:2

It's all about endings. The Torah portion describes the final tasks that must be completed in the construction of the ancient Tabernacle. In much the same way, the haftarah describes the final steps in the construction of the ancient Temple in Jerusalem. Some scholars believe that the entire account of the construction of the ancient Tabernacle was simply a way to offer a "blueprint" for the ancient Temple. Perhaps the ancient Tabernacle never even existed! But the ancient Temple certainly did—and you can still visit its remnants: the Western Wall in Jerusalem, the retaining wall of the Temple Mount, the wall that held up the entire structure.

Why Solomon? Why Not David?

It hardly seems fair. Here we have King David—a mighty warrior, a great king, a man who is believed to be the ancestor of the Messiah. You would think that he would have had the privilege of building the Temple in Jerusalem. It would have been an appropriate use of his talents.

But, no. It didn't work that way. The haftarah makes it very clear: King Solomon, David's son, built and dedicated the ancient Temple in Jerusalem. So why couldn't David build the ancient Temple? Solomon himself says as much: "Now my father David had intended to build a House for the name of the LORD, the God of Israel. But the LORD said to my father David, 'As regards your intention to build a House for My name, you did right to have that intention. However, you shall not build the House yourself; instead, your son, the issue of your loins, shall build the House for my Name'" (1 Kings 8: 17–19).

First, what is the meaning of building a house "for God's name"? How do you even do that? "Name" here does not really mean name, as in someone's personal name. No; as biblical scholar Benjamin Sommers teaches, "The shem [name of God] is only a sign of divine presence" (Benjamin D. Sommer, *The Bodies of God and the World of Ancient*

Israel [Cambridge, UK: Cambridge University Press, 2009, 62]). Whenever the Hebrew Bible mentions God's *shem* (name), it is another way of saying that people could feel God's presence. That is exactly what happens in an ancient temple or in a modern house of worship—you should be able to feel God's presence.

That leaves us with a hard question: Why couldn't David build the Temple? (You might even ask yourself: Why does God even need a temple? Can't you worship God anywhere? Good question—and people have been asking that same question, well, even before the Temple was built.)

The Hebrew Bible itself gives us the answer. Much later in the Bible we read: "David said to Solomon, 'My son, I wanted to build a House for the name of the LORD my God. But the word of the LORD came to me, saying, 'You have shed much blood and fought great battles; you shall not build a House for My name, for you have shed much blood on the earth in My sight. But you will have a son who will be a man at rest" (1 Chronicles 22: 7–8).

The answer is simple: David's hands were stained with the blood of his enemies. Solomon was a more peaceful man; in fact, his Hebrew name, Shlomo, comes from the word shalom, which means peace. The Temple symbolizes peace—peace between people and God, and peace between people and each other.

One thing is clear, however. There is a remarkable parallel to the story of Moses. Moses was not permitted to enter the land of Israel because he had lost his temper. His work, therefore, was left unfinished. David's work—building the Temple—was also left unfinished. Perhaps this teaches us that our parents and ancestors always leave to us some unfinished work: creating a world of peace and dignity.

❖ Notes

❖ Notes

CPSIA information can be obtained
at www.ICGtesting.com
Printed in the USA
LVHW08s0951050818
585984LV00004B/432/P